Happy. Humble. Motivated.

*How I Turned a 600-Dollar Investment
Into a 20 Million-Dollar Company*

Wilbur You

Dedication

To my loving grandfather, Zhu Xiang Wang, who made it all possible and paved the way for my family. The sacrifices he made will always be remembered. He was one of the most loving, selfless, and intelligent people I have ever known, and I'm forever grateful that I got to call him

Grandpa.

Chapter One

Cultural Barriers

I have no memory of my father. He died before I had even learned to speak his name.

He and my mother, Hong, immigrated to Brazil from their native China in 1990, hoping to build a better life there. But a better life would have to wait. I was born in São Paulo, Brazil on March 6, 1991. My father was killed two years later. And, while the dramatic circumstances of his death would majorly impact my life, that's not the point of this story.

After losing my father, my mother became disenchanted with Brazil. She reached out to my uncles in Chicago, who immediately packed their bags and booked a flight to São Paulo. Our path was clear: we would start new in America.

My grandpa had moved to the United States during the Cold War after a personal invitation from the President of the United States. As a nuclear physicist, his knowledge and skills were coveted, and so he settled into Aurora, Illinois, a suburb outside Chicago, with a comfortable job at Fermilab. It was a good thing, too; my grandpa's many years in America made the transition for me and my mother much smoother than it might have been. But it still wouldn't be easy.

My uncles briefly took us in upon our arrival in the United States, but shortly after, we moved again to be with my grandma and grandpa. This would be my home until I was five years old. My mother took the first job she could find, working for $5.50 an hour at a Baskin-Robbins, and thus, our life in America began.

As you might imagine, I don't remember much from my early years, but my first memories trace back to my grandparents. Grandma never admitted it, but I was her favorite. She used to watch over me during the day so my mother could work. I can't remember her smile ever faltering. She loved to cook, especially for people who loved to eat, and I was always in the mood for food. She made sure I ate whatever I wanted, whenever I wanted, so I grew up happily overfed and a little fat. I can still remember all the smells wafting from the kitchen of the homemade Chinese food she would make just for me. Sweet, sour, savory, and a little bit of spice—I can almost taste them, even now.

My grandpa loved movies. Science fiction was his favorite genre, and I was always invited to watch with him. They were American films, and that's actually how I learned most of my English. It became ritual to decode the actors' lines in my head based on context clues. Watching movies became my translation tool.

When he wasn't perched in front of a television set, my grandpa enjoyed what he called "treasure hunting" at our local Goodwill and any fleeting garage sale in our neighborhood. You could say he was a thrift store regular, spending a good chunk of nearly every weekend on a quest for something golden. And he would take me with him anytime I asked. Looking back, I don't even remember what kind of things he bought. All that stuck with me is that this man, who made a good living, kept a good job, and enjoyed a good home, was still a frugal man. He could have afforded more luxuries than he allowed himself; instead, he was content with the simple things and saved whenever he could. Perhaps you could call that being a product of his time, but the lesson made an imprint on my life.

My relationship with my grandpa only grew as the years passed. His brilliant brain came in handy whenever I needed help with my math homework. Anytime I found myself stuck on a problem, he was always there to break it down for me in a way that made sense. I always did and still do think of him as the smartest and kindest man I have ever known.

Though life with my grandparents leaves me with warm memories, my coinciding recollections of starting American school still make me cringe. I had absolutely no idea how to act around other kids. I might as well have been from another planet, let alone another country. As a Brazilian citizen with Chinese heritage, I didn't know a thing about fitting into American culture. Nothing about these kids made any sense to me. And, from the looks they threw my way, the confusion was mutual.

This is also where my dad comes in. Not my biological father, of course; the man my mom married when I was five years old. Mark Stanek. He would go on to become my biggest supporter in all my endeavors, but early in my life, he guided me in a much more important way. He helped me find "normal" as I waded through the waters of uncertainty, although it was a painfully slow process.

Growing up in a Chinese-American household, we mostly spoke Mandarin at home, save for the movies my grandpa and I would watch in English. That made my shift to American school pretty tough. If you grew up in the United States, you've probably never considered how difficult it would be for someone to adapt to the nuances of American culture. I don't think you really even notice them unless you're someone who also doesn't understand them.

Luckily, I had some help. My dad was an American.

My mother and I moved in with him when they married, both of us now citizens of the United States of America, and I spent the rest of my adolescence under his care. Without even really knowing what he was doing, my dad helped me break out of my shell. Being around my dad taught me social cues; little things, like when to smile, what was funny, whether someone was picking on me just to be mean or if they were trying to get to know me.

He also taught me athletics; how to catch a baseball, shoot a basketball, hit a golf ball. He showed me how to ride a bike. Later, he would bring me to games, and we would cheer on our teams with pride. Sports became integral to my young life because of his influence.

But he never let me neglect my schoolwork, either. Any books assigned to me in class, he read along with me, helping me think through ideas for book reports and class projects. This, too, was a little thing, but all of those little things my dad did for me would eventually add up and create in me later qualities of confidence, persistence, and teamwork. Unfortunately, as a young kid who felt entirely unrelatable, I still had a long road to travel in order to get there.

Getting through a school day was like walking on eggshells. I was constantly watching other kids, trying to learn, calculating my next moves based on their reactions. But those alone confused me. These kids were goofy and loud and free, but also usually causing some kind of chaos. And there was hardly ever any consequence that followed. That wasn't reflective of the experience that I was used to. My mother is the epitome of a strong woman straight out of Chinese culture. She's supportive, but she's tough. She's encouraging, but she's hard. She's a tiger and she expects discipline. But the American school system was the last place I saw discipline. I expected the teachers to suddenly snap, the way I knew my mom would have if I acted that way around her. But the teachers remained calm, and that confused me, too, leaving me with zero clues on how to act in this environment.

I didn't understand them, and they didn't understand me, but not just because our cultures were different. The English language was still new to me, and I could feel a barrier forming between me and my classmates. From my earliest memories, I was enrolled in a program called ESL (English as a Second Language). Not only was I required to keep up with the same workload my English-speaking classmates had, but I suffered through an additional class and all the homework that went along with it. But even after the work ESL put into helping me adjust, I still found it difficult to understand the kids around me. They were speaking a completely different version of English than the language I was learning, stuffed with what I later learned was slang, a thick cushion of pop culture references that I knew nothing about. Those words were definitely not in my ESL textbook.

Of course, being enrolled in ESL actually had a very valuable influence on my life, but I wouldn't realize that until later. Learning a new language, taking on extra schoolwork, and trying to make friends as a young immigrant wasn't exactly easy, but it may have shaped my hard work ethic. Though my schedule was busy, I excelled in school. My persistence as a student eventually spilled into my work life, where I now have an unshakeable tendency to keep going, keep trying, keep producing when others around me quit.

Over time, I learned the language and, with the help of my dad, I began to learn the culture. Even still, I didn't have much social interaction in my earliest years with anyone outside of my family. Most of my early attempts to engage with the culture around me were still met with disaster. All throughout elementary school, I was essentially friendless.

I remember one day like it was yesterday. I was in the fourth grade, on my way home from school when suddenly, a group of older kids stopped me. They weren't in my grade, so I didn't really know them, but when they started forming a circle around me, I knew to be afraid. I didn't have anything of value with me, just schoolbooks and homework, so I couldn't understand what they might want from me.

When that one kid threw the first punch, I figured it out. They didn't want anything from me. They just didn't like me. And even though they didn't know me, they saw me as someone younger, weaker, and different. That was reason enough for them to leave me beaten on the sidewalk. They didn't even look in my backpack to see if there was anything to take. That's not why they were there. They just wanted to show me that I wasn't welcome.

That was a really difficult day in the middle of a really difficult time, and for a while, I was broken over it. I felt like a complete outsider, rejected by the kids around me for something completely out of my control. I felt like no matter how much English I learned, no matter how much time I spent learning their words, their ways, their culture, I would never be anything more than an unwelcome foreigner.

I stumbled home with shattered ego, tore through the door, down the hall, into my bedroom, and spent the rest of that day crying. I thought I would never fit in, and at that point, I wasn't sure I ever wanted to. If this was the way of America, maybe it was best that I just stay out of it. And, for much of my early years, I did exactly that.

Recovery after that day was slow, as I had taken a pretty big hit to my already low confidence level, but I persisted. Thankfully, I wasn't getting beaten up every day, and most of my grade school memories consisted of what you probably remember from your youth, too: feeling awkward, misunderstanding girls, fuzzy memories of teachers and classrooms and wondering why we couldn't spend more time on the playground—you know, that sort of thing.

I also managed, despite my broken English and the awkward social encounters I endured all throughout grade school, to make a single friend in the third grade: Shawn Herrick. And, of course, we became friends over a business deal. We sat next to each other in class, and one day, he reached over and stole my gluestick right out of my desk drawer. So, I did what any self-respecting future businessman would do, and I blackmailed him. I told Shawn that I would turn him in to the teachers unless he played basketball with me at lunch. He agreed to my terms and we both held up our ends of the bargain. It wasn't long before we were playing basketball at lunch without any coercion involved, and I let him borrow my gluestick anytime he needed it. We were fast friends, then best friends, and we're still best friends today. Shawn also faithfully became the first employee of the startup I would later turn into a $20 million company, Youtech. But more on that in a few chapters.

Even with the relative success of meeting my first friend, I remained mostly a loner late into elementary school. And that reality would prove to be an important factor in one of the most memorable events of my childhood. This state of being mostly friendless, combined with a new love for video games and an unrealized entrepreneurial spirit, would lead me to one ambitious, significant, and slightly crazy experience. Who says you can't start a major business when you're 10 years old?

Chapter Two

10-Year-Old Entrepreneur

There I was, a single-friended but otherwise lone immigrant youth of 10 years old, still perfecting my English language and social skills, and looking for connection outside the walls of my family home.

That's when I discovered the marvelous world of online video games. I was immediately hooked, falling especially hard for the Role-Playing Games (RPGs). Not only did these virtual worlds have all the excitement of a normal video game—difficult challenges, fantastical realms, exciting powers—but they also came with a built-in community of other players. Real people were logging in from around the world, and they were all there for the same reason I was: to connect with others from afar while playing video games.

In a matter of days, I went from being virtually friendless to having tons of virtual friends. It consumed my free time like a brushfire. As soon as I came home from school each day, I fled to my room, tore through any homework I had, and logged in. And, as soon as I saw that progress bar go from "connecting" to "connected" and my friends list go from yellow to green, I put my headphones on, sat back, and navigated the online sphere.

You may have had a similar experience as a youth. Online RPGs became really popular in the late '90s and the game development world responded to this demand with full force. In a fairly short period of time, the options for online gaming were countless, and many of them fell into my preferred genre of RPG. Between World of Warcraft, RuneScape, and MapleStory, I bounced from one game to the next. But the one that stole my heart—and would soon become more than just a game for me—was called Lineage II.

Lineage II was developed as a massive multiplayer online (MMO) role-playing game, which basically just means a whole lot of people are all playing in the same online world at a single time and are all able to interact with each other. The game was set in a secondary fantasy world in which players controlled their own, customizable characters, guiding them through dangerous missions and leveling them up to gain better gear and powers. Players from around the world would team up to embark on raids together, traversing a labyrinth or a dungeon, taking out the bad guys, and ultimately defeating a boss at the end. You could also quest together, which meant venturing out into the game world to achieve preset objectives that were meant to help you level up or collect better weapons. There were also tons of social features within the game world, like auction houses for gear and other helpful items, virtual lounges where players could hang out, and the ability to create your own guild, which meant assembling a group of people that all wanted to play together every time they logged in.

The game was hosted on online servers, which are essentially just copies or instances of the game world. The main reason they exist is because there can only be so many people playing on one server at any given time without them completely bogging down the system. So, the game developers hosted multiple iterations of the game, normally breaking them down into various geographies. For example, one might be called the U.S. West Server and host every player in the United States who lives west of the Mississippi River.

Thanks to an extremely healthy community of gamers and more servers than ever before, Lineage II was so successful that the game still exists today. Developers were able to keep the gameplay relatively unchanged with each iteration, even though the graphics have been updated a few dozen times since the early 2000s. Or so I've heard... you won't catch me playing Lineage II anymore.

But back when I did play in the OG days of Lineage II, one of the biggest hurdles for me was the pay-to-play model, which most MMO developers at the time still considered the standard model. What it meant was that you had to pay a fee, some kind of renewable subscription, in order to access the game. Plenty of developers since then have realized that they are more successful at attracting gamers if they use a free-to-play subscription model, wherein people can download and play the game for free but have the option to pay for in-game upgrades. They actually can make even more money with this model, if done correctly.

Enter Wilbur You, enterprising youth and broke video game enthusiast. Without any allowance to boast, nor a family that liked the idea of funding a hobby that kept me holed up in my room most nights, I was at a loss. But I wouldn't be beaten down again. In fact, I like to think of myself as one of the first free-to-play advocates, even at the young age of 10 years old.

Around this same time, I discovered my increasing interest in coding, being fascinated by computers and what made them tick. I absorbed any information I could find related to web, game, and software development and, by the time Lineage II came out, I was already making some pretty strong strides in my basic understanding of web and game-based coding.

My love of coding, my love of games, and my desire to stay engaged with the social connection I had found in the online gaming community all converged, and the result was nothing short of amazing. At the age of 10, I built a free online server for Lineage II. What happened after changed my life forever.

At first just hoping to play for free, I started hosting a server that anyone in the world could log into from my bedroom computer, something that really hadn't been done before. It took off like crazy and quickly became more than my dusty, old PC could handle. I had solved the problem of having to pay for my online gaming experience, but created another issue in the process. I soon needed a bigger server. And I needed money.

So, I did what every free-to-play gaming community now does: I began coding and selling upgrades. Need a better weapon? Here are your options. Your armor took one too many hits in that last battle? Don't waste your time looking for a replacement; I've got one right here for sale. People went nuts for it. Real people were paying me for virtual enhancements to their virtual characters in a virtual world with very real money… and a lot of it.

In a matter of days, I had collected enough money from users on my server to pay for the necessary hardware that would allow my community to keep growing. I had struck gold, but like anything, if it seems too good to be true, it likely is. Several months, about 15,000 users, and $50,000 later, an envelope arrived in the mail, addressed to me. I remember my throat catching when I realized I was reading a cease and desist letter, sent directly to me from the game developer—NCSOFT.

Terror washed over me like a wave in that moment. My 10-year-old brain flashed back and forth between the irrational fear of being sent to prison and the more rational (and far more upsetting) thought of losing something I had built from scratch, something I had pride in and was likely to later fund my college education.

But on the other hand, there was definitely a part of me that felt pretty good about getting that letter. Imagine being in fifth grade and just even being noticed by a giant multinational company, let alone getting a letter from them. I was big time. I had made it. I had disrupted their business model in a large enough way that they felt the ripples… and then it all disappeared.

My parents, though impressed at my ingenuity and entrepreneurial chops, were less impressed by the illegal manner in which I expressed them. I can't blame them. It was wrong. As a 10-year-old, I'm not sure I really knew just how bad it was as I was building the server, but I certainly understood after I was forced to shut it down.

That was hard. I remember crying. I remember being angry at my parents. I remember feeling like something really important to me had been taken away. But later I realized that all was not lost. Not only did I get to keep the money I had earned from the server—which meant I had plenty of cash to continue playing Lineage II—but I also gained some really valuable lessons that I still carry with me today.

Lesson number one: even someone as unexpected as a young kid armed only with a desktop computer and a problem to solve could disrupt something as powerful as a multinational business giant, that something extremely humble could grow into something paradigm-changing. All that was necessary were a few upfront resources and a whole lot of passion and hard work. I would later forget this lesson and suffer the consequences, but that's a subject for another chapter. This lesson eventually founded the cornerstone of how I think about business today.

Lesson number two: solving big problems can only be accomplished by looking at them in a different way than how they were created. I saw the cost of playing a video game as a problem and thought, *Why not make it free?* Many years later, almost every major MMO-style game uses a variation of the model I stumbled upon at the age of 10—the free-to-play, in-game purchase model. This was just a different way of looking at an existing problem, a simple view-shift, and it transformed an industry.

But something else happened during the Lineage II experience—less of a lesson and more of a life skill that I wouldn't realize I had gained until later. Lineage II was a worldwide game, and my server, in particular, had attracted people from pretty much every developed country in the world. That meant I had the opportunity to interact with people from many different cultures, even as a 10-year-old. I gamed with them, setting up teams, solving problems, and socializing. But they were also my clients. They were on *my* server, purchasing *my* products, and that meant I had to learn how to be a consultant. I learned how these people from Brazil, Portugal, France, and other countries communicated and worked in a group. They all spoke English, but they spoke it through the lens of their culture, and in being exposed to them, I began to understand those different lenses. I didn't know it at the time, but that experience would prove to be invaluable throughout the growth of Youtech.

But this experience gave me one final boon, one that would turn out to be both a huge asset and a great hindrance for the next many years in my life. It gave me confidence, a shift that colored many of my interactions throughout high school and college. From here on out, I would no longer be socially awkward, for better *and* for worse.

Chapter Three

Newfound Confidence

By the time I reached high school, everything seemed to finally fall into place. Confidence? Check. English language? Mastered. Social skills? All of them. I was well-rounded and ready to be deployed, fresh off the confidence booster of a lifetime in my Lineage II server experience, and ready to take on the world, or at least high school.

Middle school had been much more fun than I expected. My love of playing and attending sporting events with my dad had blossomed into a true, all-around passion for sports. After I received the cease and desist letter, I put video games on the back-burner and signed up for every recreational sporting league I could find. Baseball, football, basketball; I joined them all, juggling those commitments with my schoolwork and loving every minute of it. I particularly liked and excelled at baseball. I was short-stop, but I also played pitcher, on occasion. Not only did this immerse me in a social environment with other kids my age, but it also taught me a lot about camaraderie and teamwork, two things that now contribute to my success on a daily basis.

But that wasn't all; my mother had this expectation that I practice in the fine arts, as well. I had taken piano lessons and studied classical music from an early age, and continued this practice through middle school. I fully believe my music education opened pathways in my brain that otherwise wouldn't have been accessible, as it became a creative outlet for me at a time when my brain was at its most formative. Studying and practicing music helped formulate my ability to see complex issues and boil them down into simple solutions. And, by always balancing a very diverse and involved schedule, I learned the importance of being well-rounded. Music functioned as another language, another frame-of-reference, through which to view the world around me.

There was, however, a downside. Humility was a trait I had yet to learn, and at that point in my life, I truly believed I could accomplish anything. Entering high school with that kind of confidence is a little bit dangerous, but hell, did I own it. If I had the ball, I could win the game. If I had control, I could lead us to success. I was the leader. I organized homecoming and senior prom. I assembled huge backyard football games and weekend meetups. If there was something going on that more than a handful of people were attending, chances are I was either leading the charge or right in the middle of the action. I also helped people solve personal problems. I never aimed to get caught up in all the usual drama of high school, and was typically well-liked by almost everyone I knew. People would come to me to help them hash things out. I was the go-to guy. So, throughout high school, I generally operated in a constant state of confidence.

Don't get me wrong—I'm still a very confident person, and I'm not trying to villainize confidence now. Having confidence is one of the most powerful tools any child can have. Sometimes, the only difference between success and failure in a particular course of action is the level of confidence that you proceed forward with in that venture. But confidence wasn't the problem; arrogance was.

There's a very fine line between confidence and arrogance, and I'm not a psychologist, so I'll just put this in terms of how I think both traits affected me as a young man. Confidence helped me step forward, take the ball, take the lead, and deliver, all good things for me and for others. But arrogance caused me to believe that only I, and no one else, was reliable, that *only* I should have the ball, have the lead, that only I could deliver.

This confidence spilled over into rebellion, sometimes; anytime one of my teachers told me there was only one way of doing things, it felt like instinct to do it another way. I was confident now, too, and it was much easier to get away with things as a friendly person. Rules are just guidelines, and guidelines are meant to be rewritten or ignored. But in my teenage years, that manifested in the classroom in ways I now wish I had handled a bit more tactfully. I wasn't a bad student; I just believed in pushing the boundaries of what can be done.

The real challenges actually began when I stepped beyond the artificial protections of school and out into the "real world." My charming nature didn't translate nearly as well to my various employers as it had to my teachers. And, because of this inability of mine to follow instructions without asking questions and challenging authority, I gained and lost several jobs during high school. I was not a good employee. Within two years of receiving my driver's license, I had secured four jobs, and then either lost or quit them all. My first job kept me under the fluorescent lights of a grocery store, then onto a restaurant, next a retail chain, and finally, a laser tag business. But none of these jobs lasted more than two months. All were just further validation for young me that I was the smartest person I knew, everyone else could just go pound sand.

Not having a job meant not having any money, and not having any money meant not having any gas to fill up the car, all of which caused some real challenges for a teenage boy craving freedom. Remember my tiger mom? She wasn't exactly too fond of being asked for gas money just because I couldn't hold down a job.

I believe there are lessons to be found through everything in life and, looking back on high school, I could have spent a lot more time humbling myself than exploiting my own confidence. But I also wouldn't trade my confidence for anything in the world. Having belief in your own abilities and ideas is essential for those moments when you find yourself on the edge of the unknown. Confidence is knowing that you can survive out there. But believing that you're better off journeying alone—that you don't need the input of others, that your way is the highway, and any other ideas are simply not worth considering—is where you'll fail. Unfortunately, I brushed that truth off in high school, and I would learn my lesson the hard way later.

Now, I finally get the point, and that lesson of humility and teamwork is one that has shaped how I run my business today. People like me have an innate need to lead, and truth be told, many of us can't help it. I used to see that as a fault, but over time, I realized my leadership skills didn't evolve from my ideas being better than anyone else's. They took shape because I was willing to bear responsibility for the results. Good or bad, above expectations, or sub-par, the responsibility is mine. There's strength in a team, and I always give credit where credit is due, but someone has to take the lead.

Responsibility is a shield I bring to work every single day. When things go wrong, I fall on my sword, but when things go right, I am able to pull back the shield and let my hardworking employees bask in the light of success. I am in complete control of my own destiny, but I also know that I don't have all the answers. That's where my team comes in, supplementing my weaknesses with their strengths. We work together, and that's why we succeed.

I eventually learned the difference between responsibility and credit, arrogance and confidence, hubris and humility, but it would be a while before I applied any of this. First, I had to survive the rest of my adolescence, which wasn't going to be easy for someone like me. College was a tangled web full of rules that were meant to be broken. And I was on my way.

Chapter Four

A Humbling Blow

In the summer of 2009, I left home and flew across the country to Arizona State University (ASU), where I would study business—or at least that's what I told my parents. I may have even told myself that, too, just for the first few weeks. But the truth was I hadn't made that cross-country move to study business. Sure, those were the classes I had signed up for and those were the books I had purchased in the campus bookstore. But the reality—what I knew in my gut—was that I had really just wanted independence. I love my family, and they have always been the steady rock upon which my success was built, but as an 18-year-old boy, I was ready to play life by my own rules. I went to ASU to do just that: to be on my own, finally. Business school was just the excuse to get me there.

But as soon as I arrived, I felt alone. The town was unfamiliar, the campus still a maze, the weather, unpredictable, and the people, strange. I might as well have just moved to the moon. Sadness swept over me as the first few weeks passed; that feeling of missing everything I had left behind wasn't going away. I missed my friends and my hometown and all of its familiar spots. But most of all, I missed my family, despite my newfound independence.

It wasn't long before I was aching to go home, but I couldn't just quit. The freedom was a little bittersweet, but I decided if I was going to survive this unknown place, I would have to start making friends.

So, I socialized, first making friends with a few kids from my floor, and then meeting their friends, and then their friends, and so on. Soon, it felt like I had picked up right where I had left off in high school. I was able to parley my fine-tuned social skills into an abundance of fast friends, and at the time, I saw this as an asset. Invitations to literally every event anywhere near campus were sent my way. *Eureka!* I thought. This was my in. I would survive college after all.

But, boy, was I wrong. No one told me you actually had to study in college. The movies, especially, presented college as a perpetual party, so that's exactly how I treated it. I went out, I hung out, I partied, I drank, I drank some more, I drank maybe a little bit too much, and I did all again the next night. I enjoyed college the way I thought every freshman was supposed to enjoy college. My mind was focused on all of the excitement rather than any of my homework, and that's when it all went south.

By the end of that first semester, I can honestly say I had the best time of my life with some very memorable people, but I had also failed math. *Math*. Not only had I never failed a class before, not even close, but it definitely shouldn't have been math. Maybe English. But not *math*. I loved math, and I pride myself on being good at the subject. More than that, I had always felt an obligation to master math because my grandpa had spent so much of his time helping me understand math. This blow was bigger than I could handle.

But there it was, plain as day. An "F" next to the math course on the electronic semester summary. I was shook. I felt sick to my stomach. Everything felt like it was crashing down around me, and never in my life had I missed my family so much. I made the decision right then and there to return home. My was telling me to do it and there was no use fighting it. I wasn't ready for college. I wasn't ready to live without the stabilizing influence of my family. I packed my things, said goodbye to my friends at ASU, and was on a flight back east before the weekend.

I think about that semester a lot. One of my weaknesses is pride. I have to succeed. I have to win. I have to achieve the goal I set out to achieve. I realize now that I was just a kid. I was a kid with an inordinate amount of confidence and an unhealthy lack of ability to see my limitations. Somehow, I had convinced myself that I didn't really need to try that hard, and somehow, I would get by. I thought that this whole college thing was just something I needed to pass and be on my way, and all would be well.

But I learned a valuable lesson that semester. Life doesn't care what your assumptions are. It's not going to let you just slip by without even trying, nor will it help you avoid screwing up. Life is indifferent to your confidence, and if you're going to succeed, you can't assume things are going to work out well just because you want them to. You have to put in the time. You have to put in the work. You have to assume that the thing you must do will be harder than it appears, not easier, then plan for that and work your plan.

I returned home and took a semester off from college. I spent that time refocusing on what was next for me. I had learned some hard lessons. I still had confidence, but life had dealt me a humbling blow. I was no longer a superhuman. I was just a normal guy who knew it was time to buckle down and work hard. I was done failing. I was ready to succeed, and that's what I would do. That's what I had to do. Or so I thought.

Chapter Five

The Learning Phase

My first attempt at college was behind me, a failure I had accepted and moved on from. I was back at home, back in the comforting safety of familiarity, but most importantly, I was back in control. With no debt, very few expenses, and no studies or parties to steal my attention, I took some time to think about my future with a clear head. What did I really want to do? What was I good at, interested in, passionate about? What could I pull from the recesses of my mind into the foreground that might shape what I want to do for the rest of my life?

I dug back through my childhood one memory at a time, searching for clues as to what might be a sustainable direction for me long-term. Figuring it out didn't take long when I really thought about my skills as a person. At this point in my life, I was confident to a fault and a hard worker, able to see common problems in new and unique ways. I was great at networking and building trust with others. But I was also really terrible at taking direction from anyone, which meant I shouldn't seek a job where I'm not the boss. And then it hit me. I was meant to build my own business. I was meant to be an entrepreneur. I had already found early success in that arena, albeit illegal success. Still, everything about the Lineage II server experience only reaffirmed this belief in my ability to envision, launch, and run a successful business.

Coming up with ideas is another strong suit of mine, and I consider innovation a unique gift that some entrepreneurs just don't have. They may carry all the tools it takes to be a great entrepreneur: they're self-starters, motivated, hard-working people-persons, but they lack that initial idea to get them started. Fortunately, I've never had that problem, and fresh out of my first semester at college, I had so many ideas that I needed a reliable way to narrow them down.

Ideas are invaluable things, so until I had decided which direction to take, I couldn't risk spoiling any particularly enticing projects. I spoke only to the people I trusted most, running by them my various startup concepts and quickly narrowing my list down to a winner. I would create an online advertising platform, which used images of the actual skylines of various cities as a backdrop for ad space. I would call it The City of Ads.

I was energized by the support of my family and close friends. Everyone thought it was a great idea, and so did I. I went right to work, planning, researching, reaching out to local businesses, drawing up concepts of the site, and soon, I had a rough budget of what it would take to get this thing up and running. Then I did what I thought every good young business tycoon should do: I started looking for investors. Isn't the first rule of business to never invest your own money? I knew I would need around $20,000 to give this great idea the launch it deserved, but I didn't realize how lucky I would be to find that money so easily. I hardly had to look, let alone even leave my house. My family was so supportive and enthusiastic about the business that they funded the launch in full—all $22,000 of it.

Grateful and elated, I was off to the races, buying up server space, hiring programmers, and calling local businesses that had shown interest in the idea. We were based in Naperville, Illinois, and the companies around there were salivating over this idea. Everything was lined up as it should have been. But not long after I launched, I ran into two problems. Two *huge* problems. Problems that could and should have been avoided. And both would ultimately ensure the downfall of the business.

A safe investment was my main priority when starting up The City of Ads, and I knew that meant investing someone else's money. I had done my homework. All the books implied that, too. So, when my parents offered to fund the launch, I thought I could breathe a sigh of relief. There couldn't be a safer scenario than that.

The problem was that it was never truly safe. This false sense of security clouded my vision, once again making me think I was limitless. My parents surely felt none of this false safety, since they knew better, but their love and support kept them from exposing their fears to me. They protected me from their worry, let me fly while they dealt with the consequences. And when I crashed, I felt all of the pain.

I moved into this business with a faulty outlook that there was no risk involved and I had the ability to pay for anything I needed. I should have known better.

When I built the Lineage II server, I started with nothing more than a computer, some coding knowledge, and a passion to create. That is why I was successful. I had a mindset, whether I knew it at the time or not, that I had to put in the work myself. I had to, because there was no one else. It was just me, and I didn't spend anyone else's money. I found a way to start small, build up, and make money to sustain the growth over time. If I had applied that same mindset to The City of Ads, I might be writing a very different book right now. Starting with zero dollars would have forced me to learn how to do all the things necessary to launch that business and do it right.

All was well at first. I had envisioned this incredibly elegant ad space solution that would make ads relevant to the geography in which they were advertising. Businesses were enthusiastic; they really bought into the vision, and I was able to sign a lot of them up fairly quickly. But when I tried to translate that vision into a real, functioning product, the reality fell flat. And because I had approached the problem with a plan of spending my way through it, I couldn't even translate how to solve the problems I was facing to the people who were supposed to fix the problem. I couldn't bridge the gap between the expectations set by the vision and the reality of the product. Simply put, it wasn't as good as I had promised. It wasn't as seamless. It wasn't as user-friendly. It wasn't as visually pleasing. It wasn't viable.

I had started with a vision and made promises based on that vision, but didn't have the wisdom and experience to shift that vision into reality. Soon, all of my clients were backing out, my money was spent, and I was forced to dismantle the dream I had so vividly seen succeeding in my mind. And all of that could have been avoided had I began with a mindset of bootstrapping the reality piece by piece and only bringing it to the potential market of users once I had worked out all the kinks.

The other problem, which was equally as avoidable as the first, was with how I structured the business. I had entered into a partnership. Both of us were confident, headstrong, inspired leaders, and though that meant we were both willing to work hard to achieve the vision, neither of us could agree on the nuances of the vision. We couldn't decide on a direction, and I should have known I would eventually crave total control. I need to have complete responsibility for the direction in which I am moving, and without it, I feel suffocated, frustrated, and unfulfilled.

But I ignored that need to pursue this partnership. We not only failed to achieve the vision we set, but we also had some difficulty in realizing a cohesive vision in the first place. You could call them "creative differences," though this person was never what I would call a bad partner. If I had been the sole captain of that ship, I might have been able to right the heading and successfully find port. But, by the time we were nearing the end, I was just as ready as my partner was to set the whole ship on fire and row back to safety in separate life rafts.

You might think that, with the failure of The City of Ads in my rearview mirror, I would be hesitant to venture forth with any more startup ideas. You'd be right. I was hesitant. I had gone from failing college to failing my first business venture since I was 10 years old. I'd love to pretend that these experiences had no effect on me, and I just kept chugging along, secure in the confidence that I was the world's chosen young entrepreneur, destined for greatness. But that was not the case. Failure hurts. I was hurting. I was shaken. And, for the first time in a long time, my confidence was low.

I spent a lot of time in my room after that. I played video games. I thought about the future. I thought about the past. I thought a lot about the past. I ran through the intricate details of my successes and failures in my mind, trying to piece together the lessons I had gathered into a direction for my future.

That's when my family stepped in with their unfailing support. My mom and dad must have felt burned out by the investment they made in The City of Ads, and I would have understood if they tried to encourage me to stop pursuing further ideas. They could have easily tried to steer me in the direction of a "normal job" or even taking another stab at college with a renewed expectation of focusing on my studies.

But they didn't do that. They knew me. They had watched me grow, helped me grow, saw that I was a bird and not a fish and needed to be in the sky and not the water.

So, when I finally emerged from my dungeon of doubt, the first words out of my mother's mouth weren't, "When are you going to put together a resume and start job-hunting?"

They were, "What are you going to try next?" My dad was just as supportive, as were my grandma and grandpa. And, when I told them about an idea I had circling around in my head, they didn't hesitate. They told me to go for it.

That idea was Youchers. You probably thought I was going to say Youtech, didn't you? Not yet. We're not quite there. I still had a few more learning experiences to go through.

Confidence restored, and a few more life lessons learned, I began planning my next business. The idea was similar to Groupon, only it would be based locally and eventually expand to other localities, always maintaining its local appeal in whatever market it occupied. This time I was going to start simple and small and do everything myself. I wouldn't accept any investment dollars and I wouldn't partner with anyone. I would do it my way, according to my vision, and if I couldn't do it alone, then the idea must not have been that great anyway.

Again, I planned, conceptualized, networked with local businesses, and again, I found early success. Then, just like before, not long after the launch, everything came toppling down. It wasn't that the idea wasn't good. It wasn't that the concept wasn't well-received by potential clients. I had made another huge miscalculation. I couldn't do it by myself. I, alone, didn't have the bandwidth or skill set necessary to produce the product at the level of quality that my clients expected, while doing everything else necessary to run the business. Another great idea, and another failed business.

And the lesson I learned was as plain to see as it had been before, albeit completely the opposite: I couldn't do it alone. Turned out, doing things by myself only makes sense when solving small problems. Building the Lineage II server was something I could do alone, so I extrapolated that to mean I could do anything alone. But the proof is in the result. If I was going to do something meaningful, I was going to have to learn how to work with others, and that meant I needed to plug myself into an environment where I *would* be working with others. I needed a job.

Chapter Six

Applied Research

Honestly, I wasn't as downtrodden as you might think on the heels of my second failed business. There was no lost investment to mourn—this time—and, with the help of my family, I was starting to cultivate a habit of looking at failure as an opportunity to learn valuable life lessons. And, rather than use this as an opportunity to underachieve, I was not going to quit. The next stop on the road to success was to find a job in the field, my way of doing "applied research."

I still had my sights set on building my own company, one that would grow into something meaningful and lasting. But I still had one last lesson to learn before I was ready to start my business: how to collaborate with people as equals in the workplace. I needed to get in on the ground floor at this next job, observe the day-to-day and see how employees interact. Because as it was starting to dawn on me, I had no idea how a successful business—one with a larger footprint than my parent's basement—was actually supposed to operate. That's where Invsco came in.

American Invsco is a giant real-estate development company, which grew from a startup in Chicago to a multinational developer with ongoing development in 40 major metropolitan areas around the world. I was hired on as a Marketing Coordinator, which involved helping the company manage their website, create marketing campaigns, and bring in sales during the biggest real-estate recession of the past 80 years.

In my time there, I learned a lot about the most important aspects of running a business. I learned about hard client deadlines. I learned how to function in a collaborative environment. I learned the importance of developing camaraderie with my coworkers. And I learned the necessity of having a company culture that promotes hard work but also instills pride for the workplace in you. I also learned a really important "what not to do," but I'll save that for a few paragraphs. Up next is the story of how I thought of the idea for Youtech.

One of the projects I was assigned included keeping the company website up-to-date with current development project profiles. I interacted with our web developer, explained what needed to be done, procured their services, and then made sure they did a good job. Something about this process baffled me immediately, though; the web developers' services were incredibly expensive for relatively easy work. I was still web savvy from my coding and startup days, and pretty familiar with the framework and backend structure of the Invsco company website. So, it came as quite a shock to realize that the proposals sent over from our company consultant for one-to-two hours of work would be estimated at $500 to $1,000, and sometimes more.

A lightbulb went off in the entrepreneurial side of my brain, and I immediately began hatching my next big idea. But first, I had to make sure it was viable. I had learned my lessons. I wasn't going to rush into this without testing my theory first. I would persuade my boss to let me take over the updates to the Invsco company website and, if I was right about the time investment, then I would know that I could charge much less than the consultant we were using. And that I could turn into a successful business model.

So, I went to my boss, explained the issue as I saw it with our web development consultant, and told him that I could do the updates myself. Within a few days, I fell into full research mode, and long story short, I was right. The updates were just as easy as I thought they would be and the consultant was inflating prices because, apparently, that just met the demand of the current rising market for their services. But I had disrupted a market before and I was eager to do it again.

Remember that "what not to do" I mentioned earlier? It's coming up next. I didn't have the best relationship with one of my supervisors; not my immediate boss, someone in the same department with a larger paycheck. We clashed personalities and work styles, but I didn't exactly have to report to him, so there was usually no problem. At that time, the company had completed several development projects and, on top of the daily updates I had to do, my hours were mostly spent tending to the website. One day, this particular supervisor asked me to take care of something for him, and I told him I couldn't get to it for a few days because I was focused on knocking out the updates to the website.

It's safe to say he didn't like that at all. I already had a bit of an adversarial relationship with him before his request; he had this need to feel superior to others in order to feel good about himself, and I was not a person who liked to be micromanaged or denigrated. We disagreed on more than one occasion, but that day might have been his breaking point. It may have been mine, too.

When I refused to prioritize his task, rather than either finding another person to do it or scheduling it for me later, he chose to attack me as a person.

He told me I was only good at one thing, referring to my sole focus on the website, and I could never be good at multitasking everything, like he was, apparently. And then he walked away. There was no kidding in his expression, no harmless prod that you might expect from a friend just trying to get under your skin. It was just a straight-up insult from a disgruntled person in authority, but not over me. He knew he couldn't actually demand I start the task immediately, so instead, he tried to tear me down on a personal level.

That was more than I could swallow. I couldn't let him have the last word, and I was itching to leave with my new idea by that time anyway. So, I stood, caught up to him, got his attention, and told him, "No worries, I quit." I gathered my things, said goodbye to my friends there, and walked out of that building for good. I had bigger things to attend to.

Over the next few months, I thought about that interaction a lot. Ultimately, I learned something very valuable, but first, I had to realize something important, if painful. He had been partially right. He *was* better at more things, had acquired more abilities, and honed more skills than I had, capabilities that were useful to American Invsco. I could have also been more helpful in that situation. I could have said, "I can't get to it, but let me see if I can find someone else who is available," or found another way to diffuse the situation. There were a lot of things that could have been done differently, but the most important thing I learned was that, as the owner of a business, someday soon I would have to deal with people in unpleasant situations. Maybe they had a task and screwed something up. Maybe they started an argument with someone else and I have to be the mediator. Maybe any one of a million things that can happen in a business environment that aren't always peaches and cream happened, and when those situations arise, you have to be able to execute the subtle art of stepping on someone else's shoes without ruining their shine. If you insult them. If you berate them. If you belittle them. You will lose them. They will either shrink within themselves, lose their confidence and their ability to grow. Or they'll puff up and leave, just like I did.

This last lesson was one of the most important I learned, and one I have employed and refined over time. But in that moment, I recognized my cue to leave. It was time to move on, only this time, I knew exactly which directly I would take.

I even had a name picked out.

Youtech.

Chapter Seven

100 Cold Calls

As soon as I arrived home from my newly relinquished job, I immediately started planning my new startup. Youtech was destined to succeed, I could feel it, but only I could get it off the ground. I was eager to make sure this idea came to fruition and wasn't just another dead end in a long line of "learning exercises." I felt like I had learned enough of those for a lifetime, and though I knew nothing was ever a guarantee in life, I was feeling a confidence about this idea stronger than I could remember ever having before. This was it. This was the one.

The work—designing websites—was familiar to me, and I knew I could perform it at a high level. The clients were accessible and numerous, and many, I knew, were untapped in the local market. They were successful businesses just sitting there, waiting for websites of their own, some not even knowing that they needed them. And here I was, fresh with the burning knowledge that I could solve their problem at a cost much lower than the going rates within the industry.

But I calmed myself. Sitting in my parent's basement, I ran through the lessons of the past. I wouldn't say I was gun-shy—that just isn't me—but I was certainly hyper-sensitive to the nightmare of repeating my mistakes. I knew I could do the work, but I would need help; someone on the coding side and someone on the IT side. That way, while I was generating client leads, things wouldn't have to come to a halt back at the office. But I knew I couldn't make it a partnership, either. I needed to have the ultimate say on the vision and direction of the business. It had to be my baby. I had to find a couple of people I could trust, that I believed in, and who believed in me, but would also let me run the show. My first call was automatic.

I dialed up Shawn Herrick, and before I was even done describing my vision, he was on board. I think he would have agreed sooner if I had just been able to curb my enthusiasm a little and shut up quicker. Shawn could code. He didn't have as much knowledge as I did, but he was a smart guy and I knew I could teach him what he couldn't learn on his own. But that left me with an IT position to fill. As luck would have it, a father of another friend of mine had just left his job as an IT director for a large company and so was in the market for a new career move.

I gave Frank Hilgers a call, and how I handled that conversation would set the stage for much of how I approach hiring still to this day. I had little-to-no money to offer. I certainly couldn't come to the table with any benefits, let alone a retirement program. But what I could offer was something much more valuable in the long-term. I was offering the opportunity to build something, the opportunity to start from the beginning of something big and be able to say you put your mark on it, helped shape it. That is exactly what Frank was looking for in his new position, and I learned in that call that he was exactly the kind of person I wanted to surround myself with—someone who desired more than money from their job, but fulfillment and opportunity.

So, with two rock stars now signed onto the team, I took the last remaining $600 I had in my bank account and incorporated Youtech in 2012. We set up shop in my parent's basement, using the modest equipment that the three of us had scraped our money together for—at the time, this barely consisted of more than our cell phones, a couple of old computers, a used server switch, and some uncomfortable chairs pulled up to a low table. We sat across from each other and we went to work.

And work we did. In the first few months, I set a goal to make 100 cold calls to local businesses each day. We offered low-cost web development services, even as low as $200 for an entirely made-over, brand-new website. I knew that most of them wouldn't even pick up and the ones that did would likely be short rejections, but I was not daunted. Because I also knew that if I gained even one client out of 100 calls, that would be a good day. I was relentless; respectful, but unshakable in my determination to earn their business. If they gave me even the slightest opening during the call, I would burst through it, running off all of the selling points I had memorized to convince them that they first needed a website and that they should hire Youtech to develop it for them.

When I finally experienced success, I was surprised by where it came from. At the end of a long and tiring first day of rejections, I decided to call a familiar number: my old boss at Invsco. After all, I had made lots of friends there and still had a good relationship with my direct manager. To my pure delight, it was an easy sell. He was so happy at the prospect of continuing to work with me *and* to spend less money updating the Invsco website that he committed to working with us right there on the spot. Youtech had its first client, and I was overflowing with confidence. It was a good thing, too, because up until that point, I had no idea how I was going to pay my two employees.

Those first few months were tough. Not knowing whether this thing was going to take off, but coming at it hard, day after day, anyway, takes a special kind of mental gymnastics. Sometimes we would make 200 or 300 calls before securing another small contract. By the end of the first two weeks, I had landed us only two contracts. It was tough to see the questions lingering on my only employees' faces, our merry little band held together by nothing more than hope and loyalty. I was scraping together just enough money to pay Shawn $100 per week, and Frank $200. My grandpa was even letting me use his credit card to order in fast food just to keep us all going. The two-for-five meal deal at the Burger King down the road was an absolute staple of those first few weeks.

But in the end, everything worked out. We hustled just as hard to produce an excellent product for our clients as we had to earn those small contacts in the first place. By the end of the first month, those first clients had turned into repeat work and referrals to other business contacts. Within a few short months, I was spending less time calling for new work and more time managing the work coming in. By the end of the second month, though I had yet to even start paying myself a salary, I had saved enough money to move Youtech out of the basement of my parent's home and into its own office space.

The space was a humble, two-bedroom apartment over a computer repair business, but it checked all of the boxes in my book. It was clean. It was well-lit. It was away from home. And, most importantly, it had a downtown address. We were finally legit.

Chapter Eight

Growing Pains

If I thought the first few months of Youtech were hard, the next several, and the ensuing years, were practically a medieval labyrinth. But, before long, the maze of starting a business opened into daylight, and Youtech began to foster extremely rewarding results.

Sometimes, the most important reasons for its success came from completely unexpected sources. For instance, I knew having a downtown address was a good idea, but I had no idea how important it would prove to be before we moved into that first real office location. The results were immediate. The ability to answer the question, "Where are you guys located?" with a brick-and-mortar establishment that people recognized and a zip code that they respected was enormous. Our hit rate skyrocketed. Referrals started flooding in, and after about six months in that first office space, we had already reached its capacity with just three people. We were at a decision point to either hire and keep growing or cap this thing where we're at and remain a small company. But it was a no-brainer. I never really wanted to start a small company. I had dreams of evolving an industry, changing the world for my clients, and giving people a place of work they could be proud to say was theirs.

So, we hired. But we didn't just hire to grow our volume, we hired to expand our services. I had long seen a major gap between the technology and marketing sides of web design and wanted Youtech to be the bridge for it. And for that, we needed a new kind of professional. Lauren Urban came on board as a graphic designer, and just like that, we were not only building websites, but designing them. Lauren was a recent graduate from Eastern Illinois University and, at the time of her hire, had turned down more than a few large offers from some major companies. But I sensed something about Lauren. There was something in the way she carried herself that spoke of wanting more than a paycheck; she craved fulfillment, growth, experience, opportunity. I knew we had to have her at Youtech, so I called her everyday leading up to her hire just to show her how passionate I was about the company and how much we wanted her there. In the end, she took a much lower per-hour rate to come to work at Youtech.

Because of our success over the years, we have the ability now to pay competitively. There is so much potential to earn a fantastic living at Youtech; nothing gives me more satisfaction than hearing about people who came up through the ranks and bought a house or a new BMW or achieved some other major life goal. But an important part of our hiring process is just that: starting as a content writer or a graphic designer and climbing your way up the management ladder. And, to me, that means building a dream with other people dedicated to building a dream, not just chasing the highest paycheck out of college, but doing what you love for the love of it.

Lauren is still with Youtech today. She is one of the most intelligent and dedicated individuals I have ever met and is one of my best friends. Seven years after her hire, she is also now the Chief Operating Officer at Youtech, empowering the Naperville office while I lead the ranks in Scottsdale. But that's a spoiler alert.

Back to Lauren's first days at Youtech, we also found a new office space, because we were very quickly bursting at the seams. The location we found was about 1,200 square feet—about twice as big as the one we had been in—and was also in downtown Naperville. There, we hired our fifth Youtech employee, my uncle Alan, who boasted many years of programming experience. He couldn't have come aboard a moment too soon. Around that same time, we signed our first really big contract and we were ecstatic—though, in hindsight, the amount wasn't very much. The job was a major rebuild of a website for a pretty big local brand and clocked in at a whopping $100,000. Now, you may be thinking, *Well, that was the end of all their challenges. Now they have money. They can afford to pay all of their salaries, rent, and other expenses.* I may have thought that for a moment back then, as well, but I was quickly reeducated. You see, there's this little thing called *billing*, and just because you have a big contract doesn't mean you actually have any money. First, you have to perform at least some of the work under that contract, then you have to bill them for it, and then you have to wait for that invoice to go through your client's internal billing cycle. This can cause delays often reaching several months, and that's when things go smoothly without any disputes, a rare luxury not usually the case in my industry.

Taking on a huge new project, while certainly a serious reason for celebration, was also a major logistical nightmare. We simply didn't have enough people to tackle this thing and continue to work any resemblance of normal hours, nor did we have the money to hire new people in time. So, what did we do? The answer may surprise you. Instead of trying to lighten our load, we started taking on more work. Why did we do that? Because I had an idea, and I believed that idea could help us pole-vault over the major hurdle we were facing. That idea was marketing.

Now that Youtech was a full-fledged company, I had started to envision us forming branches. In addition to development work, each branch, or department, would offer a different online marketing service, and as we expanded, there would be no limit to what we could achieve. That idea became more important than ever as we increased our workload, and I quickly recognized this as our chance to solve our current problem. I could charge for a handful of ongoing services if we offered a full suite of digital marketing solutions. We could take on a client, develop, launch, and manage an online marketing campaign for them, and then update it over time with new content. We would also keep track of analytics to show them that the website we had just built or updated for them was actually worth all the money they were paying us. And, because of this model, we could charge them in advance *and* on a recurring basis, like a subscription. That's the key, after all. Always charge in advance.

And it worked. Very quickly, I landed my first major renewable marketing contract that brought in $5,000 per month. This gave us just enough additional capital to get by until we could bill for a portion of that huge new website contract. Even with our new marketing endeavor, we still had a huge challenge ahead of us, so we all buckled down, worked the extra hours—think double your nine-to-five—ate lots of pizza late into the night, and took care of business.

That was a major hurdle for us, but we got through it just fine. The end result was a very happy client and a new market for us to expand further into. Fortunately, that became a pattern at Youtech, repeating itself many more times over the years. Right about the time we'd be running out of office space and looking for a new one, we would also find ourselves staring down the barrel of another huge project, ready to launch us into a new era of rapid growth. But dealing with these huge influxes of work did get easier. The larger you grow as a company, the better you are able to absorb and spread out those efforts among the increasing number of people on board. But even so, growth continues to be an ever-evolving challenge, and not just from a standpoint of handling workload.

Another major challenge that had never even crossed my mind when I incorporated Youtech was establishing and maintaining the right company culture. In those first few months, culture wasn't even a thought. Mission Statement? Core Values? Work Environment? I was just concerned with paying my employees at the time. The company culture of Youtech back then was just three people in a basement. We worked hard, stayed nimble in our efforts, and had fun while we were doing it. If we had a lot of work to do, we put our heads down and did it. If we needed a break, we took one. If we saw an exciting project or had a client to go after, we went after it.

But as a business grows, particularly if it has the good fortune to grow quickly, culture can be much harder to wrap your mind around and even harder to cultivate. And it's so much more of an art than it is a science that can be broken down into steps and principles. For me, the culture had to mirror the same way we felt in that basement, no matter how many people we took on or how many square-feet of office space we filled. And so, as we grew, I remained mindful of those early days. I was careful to keep my own actions centered around working hard, staying nimble in my efforts, and having fun, and in that way, I encouraged my employees to do the same. I think that's really important. Just like a child will mimic what their parents do more than what they are told, so too do employees take their cues from the boss's actions.

So, quite early on, I made a decision to become the embodiment of the culture I wanted to foster. I come in early and stay late, consistently working hard. I also take breaks when I need them. I allow myself flexible time. I still routinely go after new and exciting clients and projects, just like we did back in the early days, and motivate our leaders to do the same. I brought entertainment into the office spaces: a ping-pong table, an arcade basketball game, and others. And they don't just sit there; they get used. We hold tournaments for them, and I compete in those tournaments. For a long time, I also had a pedaling exercise machine under my desk, and I would pedal away as I took on a new project. Others in the office have stand-up desk setups, yoga ball chairs, and are allowed to use anything else that might motivate their work and inspire them to keep thinking forward.

We also have a culture of reward at Youtech. We work hard, really hard. We put in long hours and most weeks, spend more of our waking time at the office than away from it. But in turn, we also enjoy a lot of success. We offer great retirement benefits, salary, and bonuses, and set structure in place so that, as a team member gains more experience at Youtech, they should never feel like they are approaching a ceiling. We host team outings and set milestones in place to help people reach their goals. But this culture of reward isn't just gratifying for my employees; it's beneficial for me, too. Fostering an environment of hard work that pays off has helped me reap a few interesting, if unexpected, rewards along the way.

First, I now feel an enormous amount of personal fulfillment that I didn't know could come from watching someone else succeed. When I see one of my employees buy a new car or house, or have a child, or send their kid off to college, or accomplish any of the innumerable things that people set as goals in their lives, I resonate with their victory. I feel a sense of tremendous joy at their achievements—their personal achievements. I get excited when they secure a huge contract from a new client, but I also find joy in their personal growth outside the workplace. I feel that just as much.

Second, and this is just practically speaking, the more they are rewarded, the more successful I become. Does this seem counterintuitive to you? It was to me, too. I had already decided early on that Youtech was going to be a company that gives back in big ways for the contributions of its employees. But I thought that was a moral decision, a quality of life for my employees decision. But it turned out to be more than that. It turned out that fulfilled and rewarded employees work better and are more productive than silenced, underpaid ones. And the result is that when they achieve more, I achieve more, and when they make more money, I make more money. As we bake bigger and bigger pies, we'll all get bigger slices. That was a nice surprise, and I've held fast to the culture of reward ever since.

Chapter Nine

Future Expansion

What does the future have in store for Youtech? The short answer is to keep moving forward. I plan to continue expanding the company's services, both in growing what we currently offer in market share and into new services altogether. I plan to continue pushing the boundaries of what can be done to integrate technology, web design, and marketing. I plan to continue reinforcing a culture of hard work, a mindset of being nimble in our market areas and having fun while we do it. Just three years ago, the only major change I foresaw in the future of the company was a new goal to grow outside of Naperville and into untapped geographies, and now we've done it.

Expanding into another city was the most logical next step for the company and is intrinsically linked to honoring the company culture. Staying put in one office location, in one geographic area, would have had a long-term effect of eroding valuable portions of that culture for a few critical reasons.

The first is market saturation. No matter how much I hate to admit it, there will always come a time when a company, in any one geographic market, begins to approach a saturation point in that market. It's just the nature of how boxes work. There are only so many clients in your market (the box), and eventually, you will have run out of people to cold-call and referrals to receive. Diversifying your services can help and certainly has helped Youtech. When we broadened our services to include digital marketing, that not only helped us get over a major workload hurdle, but also gave our growth trajectory as a company a major leg-up. Becoming increasingly more dominant in that market can also not only help you continue to grow, but also allow you to command higher fees for the amount of effort you are spending. But even after mastering these tactics and others, you will still inevitably come to a place of equilibrium in your market, a place where you have touched every potential client, broadened your services near their logical limits, and your growth will slow to a pace that approximates the growth of the market as a whole.

This is not necessarily a bad place to be, as many successful companies grow sustainably at the rate of the market they serve, and that is a perfectly fine way to grow. It provides stability, it's easier to predict operating expenses, and there's a lot to reap from it. But honestly, it's slow. It doesn't excite me. And I'm not a big fan of things that don't get my heart racing. Confining yourself to one market is typically not where the innovators and early adopters live. It's more the haunt of those who have already been in the game for a long time and like how the game is currently being played. They don't want the game to change too much because they're pretty good at it the way it is. But I like looking at things in completely different ways, changing the rules and seeing what happens. I like turning things upside down, staying on the leading edge, and taking in what I can see from that vantage. That's exciting to me.

The other thing I don't like about a slow-growth model is that, by definition, it yields slow growth for *everyone*. It produces a company environment where the newest, youngest, most inexperienced members of your company's team have fewer opportunities to grow, blossom, and become leaders. And the reason is simple. For those at the bottom to grow, those above them have to get out of the way. This means that those above them have to either rise to new challenges in the current market or move to another one. If there is no space to move upward, then over is the only open direction, and that is what expanding geographically does for a company.

So, in 2017, I decided to open a second office for Youtech. We were five years into the incredible growth of the company and had already upgraded our office space and moved locations four times. Each time, we would wait until we were bursting at the seams before relocating. Each time, we would wait until there was enough money in the bank, so that any updates or alterations of the space we were moving into could be completely funded in cash. I had learned my lessons early on and knew I wanted to keep Youtech a zero-debt business for its entire duration. That's exactly what it is, even now.

When I was ready to expand the company geographically, I knew it was time to build an office from scratch, and now we had the money to do it. The only question was... where? This is where another aspect of the company culture came into play, the part where I lead by example. Not only did I want the emerging young leaders of the company to see how you move into a market boldly, confidently, and successfully, but I also wanted to show them that you could combine your professional goals with the goals of your personal life. When it came time for some of my leaders to move across the country for work, they knew it was going to be okay, good even, because they had already seen the boss do that.

I spent a lot of time narrowing down the new location and ultimately based it on those two main factors. Where was a vibrant market that could mingle seamlessly with the services we offer and one where I felt like we could innovate within and on the edges of those services? And where do I ultimately want to be, for me, personally? The answer was Scottsdale, Arizona. The market there was booming; plenty of growth, young people moving into the area, and yet, the cost of living was still under control, which means there was a lot of potential for more growth in the years to come. I had also lived there before during my semester at ASU, so I felt familiar with the lay of the land, still had friends there, and honestly enjoyed the beauty of the area. The Arizona heat never felt daunting; I knew we could withstand the fires, and rise.

 A year later, in 2018, we built the new location, and after eight months of leadership transition, I moved from Naperville to Scottsdale full-time. Gaining a foothold in this new market was as tangible as I'd hoped; we started by leveraging existing clients from the Naperville area that had a presence in Scottsdale, and then started taking on new clients. I still travel back to the mothership about once a month to check in, make contact with everyone, and perform a quick scan of things, but Scottsdale is now my home. We have 20 employees in Scottsdale and the fort is, once again, growing quickly, closing the gap behind the 50 in the Naperville office. But Scottsdale is just the beginning.

 It was no surprise to me that the model we had built in Naperville would translate well into other markets, but I'm not going to lie, seeing the proof of it was sweet victory. And now that we've done it, we'll do it again and again and again. We'll keep moving into new markets that we feel will translate well to our business model as the leaders of our company are ready for the challenge. We will keep offering our people those opportunities, so those below them can grow, too, and more people can find their start at Youtech. We will continue our debt-free structure. We will continue to work hard. We will continue to push the boundaries of our services in every market we face, and we will continue to have fun while doing it. We will continue to change the world

Happy Humble Motivated

for our clients and for our employees, because that's what we do at Youtech.

Chapter Ten

What Drives Me?

  I am a firm believer that for anyone to have long-term success doing anything worthwhile, they have to understand their reasons for doing it in the first place. They need to be able to articulate the "why" behind the "how" and the "what" that they do. They need to be able to answer the question, "What drives you?" There might be several answers to that question for you, or there might be a single guiding light that keeps you moving in the direction that feels right. It might be something simple, tangible, something you can hold in your hand or see right in front of you. Or, it might be more ethereal, harder to define, something that you just know is right when you see it.

  There are several things that fill my actions with purpose and keep me moving toward a goal I believe in. We've already hit on most of these drivers in previous chapters, what I formerly called lessons, but now I want to dive a little bit deeper into each one. Without these, Youtech would have quickly become just another job, and I would quickly become just another worker. I honestly don't know exactly how these rank on my internal scale of importance. My gut tells me that the scale probably shifts from time to time as I continue to grow as a person, but these are the consistent lessons that have kept me moving forward along that timeline.

  I have to provide a good or service of *value* to the world. I know that may sound pretty trite or even hokey, and it probably is both of those things. But I could not own a business that sold the digital equivalent of snake oil. I have no interest in just making money. I have no interest in pumping out a product that preys on the least fortunate in our society or takes money thoughtlessly from the most fortunate. Someday, I will come to the end of my life and I want to be able to look back on it and smile, knowing that what I achieved in my life became something of value. What Youtech offers to its clients and, through them, to the world, is a major part of that.

I have to see my clients thrive. This is certainly linked to the paragraph above, but there is a subtle and very important difference—a sense of shared success. When I embody the mindset of helping my clients prosper, it completely changes how I look at the project I'm working on for them. I approach the undertaking with a desire greater than one who just aims to create a decent product. It creates a fire inside me to do the very best possible job I can for them. It makes me feel like I have a responsibility toward them beyond the contract, and when I see them succeed because of the part we played in their journey, I get a tremendous amount of fulfillment from that. I feel like a part of that success.

I have to see my employees thrive. Nothing gives me more excitement than watching my Youtech family succeed. I want everyone who works for this company to be able to look straight up and see no ceiling above them, and I want that professional growth to give them everything they need to achieve their personal goals as well. This one mindset shapes so much of how I've approached Youtech's business model. We work hard, we stay nimble in our markets, and we have fun while we do it. I move the company forward in ways that allow people room for growth, and then I get out of their way and watch them grow. I relish every minute of that.

I have to innovate. I like to take a problem and study it, turn it around and look at it from all sides, peer past the surface and see what lives inside, really understand it, and then find what's missing in our current approach. I don't think I was doing this consciously during my tryst with Lineage II as a child; I'm pretty sure I just wanted to play the game and needed a way to make that happen. Necessity drove innovation. But as I grew older, those instincts also grew, were refined and sharpened. Failures helped to hone them as well. When I started Youtech, I had one pretty clear goal in mind: disrupt the current pricing model for web services. Since then, my goal has adjusted to focusing on bridging the gap that I saw in the industry between technology and marketing. I didn't see other companies tackling those two things in a holistic way, so I thought, *Why not me?* Now Youtech does that. Now I'm focusing on new innovations, new ways to look at what we do, and how to provide those services differently. That desire to innovate will continue to launch Youtech into the future, not to mention me, too.

I have to be a leader. And I don't mean just at Youtech. That is important, and I definitely go out of my way to be seen embodying the culture that we have set up for the success of the company moving forward. But my need to lead stretches beyond the confines of my company. Specifically, I have a dire need to be seen as an example of what is possible for my generation. There are more than a few demeaning perceptions about millennials, the two most common being that we are entitled and lazy. I aim to break those stereotypes down and replace the rubble with a better example. There are certainly some lazy and entitled millennials out there, and that's a shame, because I think the vast majority of us are coming from a place that is more focused on living a life of fulfillment. We have an expectation of life that encompasses more than just survival and reproduction. Instead, we are changing and advancing the world in ways that will remain valuable to future generations. I want to be an embodiment of that, both to show the critics what my generation is capable of and to show my generation what they can do if they put their minds to it.

Chapter Eleven

Keys to Success

Look, I'm twenty-eight years old and I've only been legally able to drink for about seven years. I was born right around the time the Berlin Wall was being torn down. I know I have a lot of life left to live and a lot of lessons left to learn. I also know that any wisdom I've gained over the years is not new, but just a reincarnation of age-old truths being passed down through successive generations of would-be entrepreneurs. But I also know that the same story can truly never be heard twice. There will always be a new lense through which to see the world. Our culture, our backgrounds, our experiences all make up the way we see the world. Immigrating to the States, struggling through cultural nuances, trying to adapt to the common workplace, and then realizing I could make my own way if I just pursued a good idea all impacted the way I have shaped my American Dream. And I will tell the same story differently than you would because my life experience has been different than yours, and you will hear it differently than another person for the same reason. We can only speak with the words we have and we can only hear through our own ears. And for that reason, I believe it's important for us to keep retelling these stories of gained wisdom in our own words. So that's what I'm going to do in this chapter. These won't be groundbreaking new strategies for launching a successful startup, but they will be truths that worked for me and why, in my own words, because those are the words I have.

If you're a bird, don't try to be a fish. This one might be a little harder to put into practice than it first appears. Be yourself, sure, but it's not really that simple. We all change as we grow. We have strengths, weaknesses, good habits, and bad habits that constantly evolve as life deals us more cards. Embodying those characteristics isn't what I'm talking about here. I mean those little quirks that are intrinsically you. It's not always easy to discern these from the others, but I'll give you a few examples from my life. I have a need to do things differently. This is a fire that burns in me, and I have no power to change that. This is an intrinsic quality of Wilbur You and from it stems some weaknesses, like having a difficult time being told what to do, and strengths, like desiring to innovate. Both of those habits issue out from my need to do things differently, but they are not the need itself. Understanding that drive and learning how to harness it is a fundamental piece of my success. My first run at college was under the pretense of doing what I was "supposed to be doing." For me, that was only a recipe for failure, because it meant I was only doing what society, or my family, thought I should be doing. I went back to college later because I finally had a reason: I wanted to gain some knowledge about computer technology so that I could learn how to do things differently. I was doing it for me and who I was and what I wanted to gain from it. I had learned that I was a bird and finally stopped trying to swim.

Hire the right people. Yeah, duh, right? But I don't think we, as employers, put enough effort into choosing our hires most of the time. We hire people that look really good on paper, but don't always fit the bill from a personality or aspiration standpoint. I have been fortunate to find people who are hungry for the same destiny I am, and it has been critical to the success of Youtech. These people value working and playing hard, unlimited growth, both upwardly and outwardly, and an integration of passion for life and work. But as wonderful as these people are for my company, they might be totally wrong for yours. I think we sometimes put too much focus on what a person's paper talents are when we're hiring them and not enough on what their intrinsic capabilities are. Are they passionate? Do they have a potential to learn? Can you see them leading in some or multiple capacities? If these things are important to a candidate's future at your company, you might solve the hiring equation more heavily when comparing these factors early on. I would much rather hire someone with no relevant experience, but a huge aptitude for learning and growing. So many of the people that joined Youtech early on are now doing jobs that are completely different than the ones they were hired for. That alone is a testament to the strategy of bringing the right people aboard and focusing on their potential rather than talent.

The client relationship is everything. Clients, just like your business, are nothing more than a collection of people. You make mistakes, they make mistakes, we all make mistakes. And often, the difference between getting fired and getting another chance with your client hinges on how good of a relationship you have with them. People want to work with people. They want to know why you do what you do as a consultant and they want to feel like you are eager to know why they do what they do. You can bet they have a reason, a possibly very straightforward "why." Do you know what it is? I do everything in my power to learn my client's businesses inside and out so that I can serve them in the best way possible. I like to think that I want them to be successful even as much as they want to be successful. And, when I make a mistake, which inevitably happens at some point in every long-term client relationship, I make sure that their experience of me fixing that mistake is just as excellent as their experience with me under any other circumstances. I'm not telling you to be fake or learn a few things about your client's kids so you can parrot that back to them when you're in their office. Be real with them; trust me, they can smell insincerity as well as you can. But always give them the confidence that their company is in the best hands when they rely on you as a consultant.

Do everything you can in-house. This one might rub a few people the wrong way. There is certainly a lot of contrary advice floating around out there, claiming that growing quickly entails outsourcing the tasks that aren't a part of your core business. I'm not necessarily saying they're wrong, and there are many paths up the mountain. But learning how to do everything that I possibly can and taking those things on in-house—at least at first—has allowed me to make sure that I'm consistently delivering on the quality promise that I make to my clients. Sometimes that means hiring someone who already has experience in a particular niche of your market that you're eager to branch into. Sometimes it means identifying someone within the company who has the passion and aptitude to take on a huge learning curve and become the guru for a whole new aspect of the industry. We have even hired people on a commission-only basis because of a certain skill they brought to the table. However you do it, I think you'll find that there is a real benefit to welcoming additional skills into your business, rather than trying to manage someone remotely. Even if you decide that you don't want to be in the business of *fill-in-the-blank*, you are likely to learn how to better manage an outside consultant once you know the ins and outs of having tried it in-house yourself.

Burst at the seams before you expand. If you're a businessperson who has been around the retail or restaurant industry at any time, you've probably heard this mantra as it relates to occupying square footage at a location. As the theory goes, it's better to cram a 2,000-square-foot operation into a 1,500-square-foot space than the opposite for several reasons. Firstly and frankly, square footage costs money, so why pay for it if you don't have to? Secondly, appearing full and busy makes for much better optics to a potential customer walking by than appearing empty and slow. But what is equally important is applying this strategy to your employee base. Having too much work for your current staff is always better than having too much staff for the work. I promise you, there is always a way to get the work done on limited staff, but you can't always find a way to pay staff when you're still waiting for the work to come in. Ever since I brought Shawn and Frank on board to the my-parent's-basement version of Youtech, I have held firmly to the strategy of not hiring until I have the contract in place that will keep the new hire busy. Is this a perfect concept? Of course not. There are always the pressures of feeling like there is too much work to go around and we're constantly learning how to better manage that as a company. But as I said, that is a far better problem to have than strategizing on who we can let go because we over-hired.

Plan, move, evaluate, plan, then move again. The key to that line is *then move again*. Have you ever done anything perfectly the first time? Did you start walking the first time you stood up as a baby? Did the frisbee float perfectly toward your sibling or parent the first time you tossed it? Did you understand every math concept, master every dance move, hit every note, pluck every string perfectly on the first try? I'm guessing that none of those questions returned a "yes." I'm also guessing you eventually did learn how to walk. And maybe you aren't perfect at any of those other things, but you're probably a lot better at them now than when you started. So, why are there areas in our lives that we get excited about, fail at once, then never try again? Life sometimes feels like a long journey, and yet, it's also incredibly short. Shouldn't we give it a fair shake? By the time I turned 22, I had failed out of college and three of the four businesses I had started no longer existed. But that fourth one, though, that was Youtech. What if I had quit after my Lineage II server experience? What if I had quit after failed business number two or three? If you want to do something, you have to be willing to fail at it, fail again, and then likely a few more times before you start to feel something that resembles confidence. If you keep at it, pretty soon, those failures will start to feel like something else completely. When asked if he was disappointed in a string of failures while trying to invent the lightbulb, Thomas Edison famously said, "I have not failed. I've just found 10,000 ways that won't work." He kept moving forward, and we're obviously all the better for it.

Work harder, and *smarter* will take care of itself. I tire of people who tell others to work smarter, not harder, then duck around the corner without giving them any inkling of how to apply that to their situation. As if, by hearing that mantra, all their woes will be solved, and they'll be able to get two days worth of work done by lunch and go home happy. The truth I've relearned throughout my whole life has been that the understanding I gain from spending my time working harder teaches me how to work smarter, not the other way around. You can't flip a switch or change your mindset and, one moment later, suddenly know how to work smarter. You have to put in the work. There is no shortcut here.

Understand your "why." We talked about what drives me in the last chapter, and I count this as one of the most important aspects of sustained success. If you don't know why you do what you do, you won't be able to explain that vision to new hires and develop a cohesive culture. You won't be able to explain it to clients and build that relationship. Most importantly, you won't be able to articulate it to yourself on those days when your bed feels really good and all you want to do is sleep in a little longer. Learning what motivates me has helped me, time and time again, through the difficult hurdles of growing a business from the ground up.

Take your education seriously. And notice I didn't say college. Education comes in many forms; college is only one of them. Maybe that structure isn't for you, but you are great at self-learning through books, podcasts, news, YouTube, and the like. Maybe you prefer hands-on vocational studies. The important thing about education, in whatever form you search for it, is that you own it. You do it for you and for your own reasons. You go into it with a clear goal and move toward that goal. If you ever have the misfortune of financial disaster in your life, you may have to suffer through the terrible experience of having hard-earned possessions taken away from you by your creditors. But one thing that no one can ever take away from you is what's in your head. You get to keep that forever. Invest in your education and it will invest in you.

Listen with humility. You've already surrounded yourself with people who are smarter than you for a reason, so now listen to them. Really listen to them. This isn't something you tell others to do in the conference room meeting and then go on about your business, believing you are the end-all, be-all of good ideas. Believe me, humbling myself and admitting that other people can contribute to the success of my company has been a constant struggle for me. But the more I focus on listening to my employees and applying their innovative ideas, the better Youtech is for it.

Have a mindset of readiness. It is rare that a person's big moment happens when they are fully prepared for it. Mine sure didn't. I had just failed a college class, started and dismantled two businesses, and went to work for someone else for the first time since high school. I wasn't looking for a big break, but when the lightbulb went off, I cultivated a mindset of readiness so I could set my dream in motion. I sure didn't know everything I needed to run a $20 million business, but I accepted the challenge and hoped that I'd be able to figure it out as I went. I'm glad I did.

Give back. I'm not just saying this from an altruistic viewpoint, even though that is also extremely important. When you give back to your staff, you almost always create even more opportunities for yourself. What happens when you mentor someone in your business? Most of the time, they start taking responsibilities off of your shoulders, and they benefit by growing while you free yourself up to do some more growing of your own. Win-win.

Youtech is only just beginning its trek into an abiding era of success, and through it all, I stay humbled. Investing in the right people, knowing what motivates me, and finding happiness in my work—these ingredients make up my perfect business. The disclaimer remains, as plenty of others have succeeded differently, but my methods continue to stay true for me. That's the American Dream, after all, isn't it? Owning the freedom to pursue your own way, capitalize on opportunities, make that bet and blend a whiskey sour you'll sorely need when life gives you lemons. Take it back like a champ. Roll the dice and try again.